What the Church Should Know

LESSONS FROM AN OUTLAW BIKER

What the Church Should Know

LESSONS FROM AN OUTLAW BIKER

ROGER BENNETT

Cover designed by David Berthiaume
Text designed by Greg Solie • Altamont Graphics

ISBN: 978-1-62847-677-4

CONTENTS

CONTENTS

DEDICATION

I would like to dedicate this book to My Lord and Savior. Without His hand over me, and without His grace and mercy I would not be alive today. There's no doubt in my mind that I could not have learned these lessons, nor could I have started walking the walk, had the precious Holy Spirit not guided me.

To Pastor Terry Tomlinson and his wife, Deborah—You had the wisdom of God to allow me to study God's Word, and then you gently led me to find the truth of that Word. You taught me to study to show myself approved and taught me that God's Word is it's own best reference.

To the many other Christians who God has brought into my life to influence my walk.

To my wife Donna and my children Nicki, Angie, and Josh who have put up with my growing pains as a Christian. You have endured my best and my worst. I am thankful you have stayed with me as I have grown. I know it has not been easy. I love you all very much.

—Roger Bennett

INTRODUCTION

I'd like to start off by saying that though I may sound critical of the church, I assure you that this is not my intention. I feel grieved in my spirit concerning the condition of the Church. I believe that many Christians and Pastors know that something is not quite right, that something is missing in their personal walk and in their experience within the Church. My desire is that this book would awaken us to what we are missing, and help to guide us, with the power of the Holy Spirit, to take the necessary steps to do what is needed in order to strengthen the church and make strong disciples.

The book of Revelation directs our attention to the problems of the last day Church in chapters two and three. In Rev. 3:14, John's revelation of the Church of Laodicea shows a Church that is "missing the mark" as far as being effective in what God has called them to do. We see a church that needs to make some corrections or it will no longer be relevant to the lost world. It is a church that is called to repentance; a church that seems to have everything that it needs materially, but has left the Lord Himself standing outside looking in, not inviting Him to be a part of their ministry.

In writing *What the Church Should Know: Lessons from an Outlaw Biker,* I wanted to share how the lessons I learned as a member of an outlaw biker club have helped me in my Christian walk. I have found these same lessons throughout the Bible, *but not in the Church!*

What the church should know doesn't mean that the Church should have a head knowledge. The standards I'm sharing are basic core teachings and beliefs that they do know, but very few individuals in Churches put them into practice themselves, and they are rarely taught to congregations.

These are principles such as loyalty, commitment, your word, no excuses, and many other practical standards that the Lord has set for the church. But the church by and large has cast off many of these teachings for the sake of having numbers. Many in the church have compromised the gospel message just to please people and to get church rolls to climb. Compromising integrity and beliefs is something that an outlaw bike club would never do in order to get people to join.

I have seen a shocking thing among the Churches: As they grow in number, they decline in Spiritual power. They are larger, but weaker. Sadly, the larger churches have become role models for the smaller ones, and rather than follow the Word of God, they model their Churches after the larger ones.

As a result, many large *and* small Churches have no power, and no conversions to the faith. Churches are stealing members from one another instead of converting the sinners.

My intent in writing this book is to show that if some heathen outlaw motorcycle clubs can have their act together and have an influence in the world while keeping their clubs free from outside (non biker) influence, then we should be able to do this in our Churches. If they can hold firm to a set of rules and standards that have been set for them because of their love for motorcycles and lawlessness, then we, as the Church, who claim to have a love for God and His set of standards (The Bible), should be able to surpass their loyalty and obedience by the guidance of that Book and the leading of the Holy Spirit.

It is time for the Church to shake itself and wake up to the fact that if we don't get our act together, there will be many condemned to an eternity without hope and without God. I believe that the words Jesus spoke when He said He would build His Church and that the gates of hell would not prevail against it (Matthew 16:18) are all true. I also believe His words that "...small is the gate, and narrow the road that leads to life, and only a few find it." (Matthew 7:14).

We need to become the Church that helps lead people along the narrow path and through the strait gate. Let us get our act together so we can be a worthy example to follow.

In my years as an outlaw biker, I found certain rules to be true. These rules applied to everyone in the club: you had respect for one another, you made no excuses, and you were willing to die for what you believed. If these things were not a part of your life, the club could not be a part of your life. The most important thing was that you were ready to put everything, as well as everybody in your life, on the second shelf, and the club came first. No exceptions!

I desire that this book will inspire us as Christians to put God first, to have a respect for Him, His Word, and one another as fellow laborers and as a family of believers. I'd also like it to teach us that when it comes to obeying God, we cannot have excuses. And finally, it's my prayer that we would become willing to die for what we believe. All of these principles are biblical and required by God—He is all of these to and for us.

Throughout this book you will notice that I refer to the motorcycle group as a club, rather than a gang. The reason for this is that while in the club, a gang was regarded as a group that has no organization. The club was very well organized; therefore it was never a bunch of rag tags without control, direction, or strong leadership.

—Roger Bennett

CHAPTER ONE
FAMILY
The Patch Holder

"God sets the lonely in families...."
—Psalm 68:6

What is a Patch holder? This may be a question on your mind, so let me explain. When an individual finally passes all of the preliminary steps to join an outlaw biker club, such as the hanging around which is the process of hanging with club members for a time at different club functions or at bars where club members frequent and the prospecting periods. This is when you are invited by the club to be a prospective club member. I will talk about this in later chapters. A member then receives a three-piece patch. This patch consists of a bottom rocker, which denotes the name of the town your chapter is in, a top rocker which has the name of the club you belong to, and a center patch which is the logo of the club itself.

The goal of every prospective member is to receive this patch, also referred to as his colors. When a person becomes a patch holder it makes a statement to other outlaw biker club members. It says he belongs to the family of bikers known as *whatever the club name may be.*

Families have always been important to God. One of the first institutions that God established was the family. When God created Adam, He said that it was not good for him to be alone, so God created his wife, Eve, and gave them directions to be fruitful and multiply. The family was born. It gave both of them as individuals, a sense of belonging, and neither were alone.

Being a member of a motorcycle club, or any other organization gives a person a sense of belonging. It gives a feeling that no matter what happens, there's someone to help, someone to lean on, and someone to give boldness and comfort. Whether it is a motorcycle club, street gang, or a social club, we see the fellow members as extensions of a family.

In a family, the members are to become one with each other, which means that they give themselves to one another. All that they are and all that they have are for each other, even laying down their lives for each other. John 15:13 says, "Greater love has no one than this: to lay down one's life for one's friends." In John 15:12, Jesus admonishes us to "Love each other as I have loved you."

In the club it is expected to put others before yourself. What a great biblical concept for a bunch of non-believers. Paul said it this way in Philippians 2:3, "Do nothing out of selfish ambition or vain conceit. Rather, in humility value others above yourselves." In the church we often find the opposite—we find pride and selfishness.

A biker club member would honor the name of his club by never doing anything that might bring embarrassment to the organization. The members would never be caught fighting amongst themselves, and they were expected to constantly live according to the family heritage.

Each member of the club is held accountable for their lifestyles, their attitudes, as well as their responsibilities. This is something the church today should do, but often does not.

The church today needs a call for right living, so as not to dishonor the name of Christ and the family of God. Rarely is Church discipline spoken of or practiced in this day and age, and there does not seem to be an expectation for its members to live godly lifestyles.

In the club there is no such thing as compromise. Each club member is expected to live like one in thought, word, and action. Conversely, the church has little to say about living without compromise or about living a righteous life.

When I received my membership in the club, it meant a great deal to me. It was special because of what I had to go through to belong, and because of the demands placed on me even before I could become a member. In Churches today, many Church members don't see membership as something special. They have not had demands placed on them before becoming members.

Before joining the club, they gave me time to count the costs of belonging to this family of bikers. I knew this process needed to be taken seriously because once a man joins the club, he's in it for good. Once you are accepted as a member, the only way out is by death. It was only by a miracle of God that I was able to get out when I did. Some may be beaten and thrown out. Some, they may allow to retire in good standing but this is very rare and must be approved by the board. Before becoming a prospect, one of the members sat me down and explained that by joining the club, I would be asked to put the club before my family and friends. I would be asked to lay my life down for the club, and if the time came I'd even have to give up my freedom for the sake of the club. These were serious issues, and the cost had to be counted before joining.

In Luke 14:25–33, Jesus stresses the importance of counting the cost before building a tower or going to war. This is a very important part of entering a covenant. In Jewish culture, when a person wanted to enter a covenant with another individual, there were certain steps that had to be taken.

It went something like this: If I was considering entering a covenant with someone, I would have to recognize that if he had any enemies, they would become my enemies. If he had any debt it would become my debt. What was his would now be mine and what was mine would now be his. So I would count the cost and see if this was a situation I wanted to get myself into. In the Church today, the cost and the requirements of membership are hardly ever explained before an individual joins. As a result, they do not realize just what they are getting into or what is expected of them or from them. Without explicit expectations, they cannot count the cost of being a Christian before joining the Church.

The next thing that would happen in a covenant agreement is that the elders in the city would call a solemn assembly at the city gates, and the two entering the covenant would make a public announcement that they were entering a covenant together. Then they would exchange robes, and an animal would be cut in half. Next, the two entering the covenant would walk between the halves while saying, "If I ever violate this covenant may the same thing happen to me that has happened to this animal." All these steps were vital in the initiation of a covenant. If any part was left out, the covenant became void.

In the Church today, when we want to get people to enter a new and everlasting covenant with the Lord, we preach messages that work on the emotions of an assembly, then everyone is asked to bow their heads. With nobody looking (in an effort not to embarrass anyone) an appeal is made asking for individuals to give their lives to Jesus.

There has been no cost counting and no public announcement made when entering a covenant. People don't want anyone to see them make a commitment, and it's treated as an embarrassing thing. What is wrong with this picture? *Remember anytime any part of the covenant act is not followed through there is no covenant.* Before making a covenant in this situation there's no counting the costs nor are there witnesses to this agreement.

Today there are many who think they are saved, but they aren't. They try to live the Christian life under their own power, and after a while they fall away. Then the Church wonders what happened to them. People begin to ask "How come they went back to their old life?" They actually never left it!

Often, when talking with one of these former Christians who are living in sin, we tend to say, "What you need is Christ." They usually will reply saying, "I already have Him."

If we were to then ask "How did you come to know Christ?," they will tell us that they were in Church one day, and the preacher had everyone close their eyes, and all who wanted Christ were to repeat after him, and that's what they did. Trying to convince such a person that they aren't saved is nearly impossible. A result of these types of appeals is that we make people into two-fold children of hell, because now it will be almost impossible to get them to believe that they really do need Christ or to see that a one time commitment does not make someone a Christian. The church today has confessions in the dark, but no conversions to the Light

When I became a member of the club—a full Patch Holder, I was not ashamed or embarrassed. I wore my colors with pride for everyone to see. And later, when I became a Christian, I wore those colors with pride just as well. In my earlier life, everyone knew I was a biker and now everyone knows I am a Christian. I never tried to hide either, and I was never ashamed or embarrassed by either. I was proud of my life change from a citizen (non-biker) to a biker and I am proud of my life change from a dead man and a sinner to one who received a new life and forgiveness of sins.

In the club you could never get away with pretending to be a patch holder. But in the Church, people try to get away with pretending to be a Christian. They may fool other people— maybe even the Pastor. However, they are not fooling God.

In the club we had many who hung around us, whom we called wanna bees. They wanted to be like us, but would not make the commitment. They liked being associated with us, but would never take on the whole lifestyle. Oh, they had the motorcycle and the lingo, but not the Patch (colors). There are many in the church today who are wanna bees. They have a Bible and the Christian lingo, but not the lifestyle, not the personal walk. They don't belong to the family because the cost is too high. It costs your whole life.

The first thing that has to happen is counting the cost, deciding in your heart whether the body of Christ is the family you want to belong to. Is it worth the cost of letting go of the old and putting on the new, making the exchange of our filthy rags for His robe of righteousness, proclaiming Christ, allowing Christ to put His patch on us—The seal of the precious Holy Spirit, and leading others to become part of this great family of God?

To some people it is frightening to think about becoming a club member. To some it is frightening to think about becoming a true Christian. Remember this life is available to anyone but not accepted by everyone. "For many are invited, but few are chosen." Matthew 22:14

CHAPTER TWO
YOUR WORD
No Excuses

"All you need to say is simply 'Yes' or 'No'; anything beyond this comes from the evil one."
—Matthew 5:37

When I was in the club, one of the most important lessons that I learned was keeping my word. In the club, one's word is everything—and if you did not keep your word you were considered a liar. It was counted as character, and is a very strict standard. The club members needed to know that you could be depended on in a life or death situation.

If members of the club would not keep their word, it made the whole club look bad. When dealing with other clubs, it was important that they see your own club members as trustworthy.

If you told someone you would be at a certain place at a certain time you had better be there. The only excuse was that you were in the hospital or dead, and unfortunately if that were not the case it would be, if you get my drift. Generally people who would not keep their word were found out during the prospect period and they would never get their colors. They never got to join the club. In most cases they would forfeit their bike and anything else the club wanted to take. They would in all cases be beaten severely as well.

Unreliable members were not allowed. If, after becoming a member, a man would start to show signs of being undependable, he would be stripped of his colors and again dealt with rather harshly. No one wanted to lose his patch or even a part of it. Losing a part of your colors meant lost position and authority, and there was nothing more humiliating.

There was no such thing as an excuse, they heard them all, and listened to none of them. Even a bike braking down would not be an acceptable excuse. The only thing that counted was reliability.

So how does this apply to the church? Matthew 5:37 is a powerful reminder to us as Christians that God wants us, His children as members of his family to keep our word. "Simply let your 'yes' be yes, and your 'no' be no, anything else is of the evil one." If you aren't sure that you are able to do something, you are better off not saying that you will. If you don't think you can keep an obligation, better off not making one. Not only is it a poor reflection on you, but more importantly it makes the body of Christ look bad and unreliable to the rest of the world.

A sad reality today is that many Christians have ruined the reputation of the Church and made a mockery of Christianity. How many times have we heard that Christians can't be trusted, they don't keep their obligations, and on and on. I have a friend who owns a music store, and he will not give credit to Churches or Christians because many times they have not kept their word. "Let your 'yes' be yes and your 'no' be no!" Many times when a Christian says he will do something, he really means he might. If he says he won't do something, it means he might not. This is supposed to be basic Christian principle. If the church can't do something as simple as keep their word, what are we headed for?

In Luke 14:15-24 Jesus tells the story of the great supper. One by one they all began to make excuses, and not one of those men who were invited, ever got a taste of the banquet. We don't have time to make excuses, and we don't have reason not to keep our word.

Remember in the club how a person would be dealt with severely if he didn't keep his word? How do we think God will deal with those who do not keep their word? Not keeping one's word is lying, and Revelation 21:8 says that all liars have their place in the fiery lake of burning sulfur. Sadly there are even pastors who have proven themselves untrustworthy. This has helped to malign the word of God.

In the club, you'll also remember part of the discipline was to lose a part or your entire patch (colors). These could be lost in increments; meaning one piece at a time or all at once, depending on the severity of the deed. This was not just humiliating; it was also a matter of losing position and authority. A person who was in the club for a long time could be brought back down to a prospect, or worse—kicked out of the club altogether.

Think about this in the spiritual realm—we lose position and authority when we don't keep our word. The devil loves that. He is a legal beagle. He knows that those who violate scripture are trespassers who have gone against what God's Word has said. The devil knows that trespassers will be prosecuted. In other words, he has got them.

So what do we do? Let us be men and women of character. Let us keep our word, our integrity, and our authority. There is strength and righteousness in this. Give thought to your words and your commitments. Think before you speak. Let your word be your bond, so honor and integrity can be restored to the body of Christ, His church, His people.

Excuses

I would like to say just a few more words on the subject of excuses. I know this is a delicate subject since we all have so many of them. We even have excuses we have not used yet, but given the right opportunity, look out.

I once heard an old Chinese proverb that goes something like this: A Chinese farmer went to his neighbor and asked if he could borrow his plow, because his was broken. The neighbor replied that he could not lend it to him, because his wife was combing her hair with it. The farmer, stunned, said "Your wife is *combing her hair with a plow?!*" To which the neighbor answered, *"No, but when you don't want to do something, one excuse is as good as another."* Many times we may think that our excuses are good ones, but the fact is that there are no good ones. One man says that an excuse is just a lie covered in the shell of reason.

If we truly believe that something is important enough, we will make time for it. It is when other things come in and take priority that our commitment levels change. Then we feel the need to make excuses. That is why in the club there is no room for excuses. If you made a commitment yourself, your following through was of the utmost importance. The bottom line was, can your word be trusted, and is the business of the club on the top of your priority list?

Your time will reflect what you're committed to. That is why in Luke 14:15–24, when Jesus told the parable of the great banquet, it was in part to challenge the level of commitment to the things of God and the kingdom of heaven. Notice that all of their excuses only served to make the master of the house angry. Not one excuse was acceptable—not the one dealing with their property, not the one dealing with their possessions, not the one dealing with their personal family life. Yet in our carnal nature, we think that the things of God can be passed off with an excuse.

How many times have we told the pastor we would be there, and when the time came, something else took priority and we made excuses? How many times have we volunteered to serve in the church, or even told God we would do something, then made excuses when it was time to fulfill the commitment? This is no different than saying,

"I am combing my hair with my plow."

What would we do if we could not trust God to keep His word with us? Could you have faith in a God who is unreliable? One who has no real commitment to what he has promised? We are created in His likeness and image. Let us strive to become like Him in every aspect of our lives. There are no areas of our life that God wants to leave unchanged. If making excuses bothers God, it should bother us as well. Let us allow God the privilege of changing us—no excuses.

CHAPTER THREE
UNITY
All on One and One on All

*"How good and pleasant it is when
God's people live together in unity!"*
—Psalm 133:1

Unity is one of the strongest forces in the universe. The club knew it had not only to establish, but also to maintain unity. If we could stand together, we could stand against anything or anybody. Disunity was one thing that would not be tolerated. The club officers knew that if unity could not be kept, the club would not survive.

The club was very well organized. There was an executive board made up of the head, called the USA. The USA was the president over all the chapters of the club no matter where they were located. He oversaw every chapter of the club across the country. Then there was the Vice President, Secretary and Treasurer, the Sergeant of Arms and the Enforcer, along with the other members of the board of Directors, which was usually made up of chapter Presidents. Each chapter had almost the same make up as the national board, so they could govern themselves to a lesser degree.

The club was organized in this way so that they could maintain order and unity. Let us focus on one particular board, or chapter member—the Enforcer. His job was to enforce the club rules and standards set by the national board. Each member and each chapter were held to the same standards. The reason for doing this was for the club to project to the public that it had no problems within the organization. The club felt it very important for no discord of any kind to take place amongst the brothers.

One of the jobs of the Enforcer was to stop fights or arguments from taking place in public. The club wanted the rest of the world to believe that they were so unified that nothing could separate the brothers. If someone outside the club fought with a club member, he would have to fight the whole club.

If any member got out of line with another member, the Enforcer would quickly put an end to it. The dirty laundry of the club was never aired in public. The dispute would later be dealt with in the privacy of a chapter meeting, where it could be decided who was responsible for the discord. It would be in one of these chapter meetings that the punishment for causing discord would be decided on. It could range from losing a piece of your three piece patch to being beaten and thrown out of the club depending on the severity of the fraction.

1 Corinthians 6:1–7

If any of you has a dispute with another, do you dare to take it before the ungodly for judgment instead of before the Lord's people? Or do you not know that the Lord's people will judge the world? And if you are to judge the world, are you not competent to judge trivial cases? Do you not know that we will judge angels? How much more the things of this life! Therefore, if you have disputes about such matters, do you ask for a ruling from those whose way of life is scorned *in the church*? I say this to shame you. Is it possible that there is nobody *among you* wise enough to judge a dispute between believers? But instead, *one brother takes another to court—and this in front of unbelievers!* The very fact that you have lawsuits among you means you have been completely defeated already. Why not rather be wronged? Why not rather be cheated?

Often times this is not how the church deals with matters amongst the brethren, instead we talk about issues to unbelieving friends and family. This is disunity pure and simple done in front of unbelievers. How unfortunate that there is broken unity, but even worse is the fact that it is happening in front of the unbelieving. Many today do not realize the bad example the church sets for unbelievers when acting in this manner. It also opens the Church to criticism from both unbelievers and believers alike.

Think of what Paul said, "Why not…be wronged? Why not…be cheated?" The fact that there is disunity means "You have been *completely* defeated." Did you get that? When we as a church air our dirty laundry in public, we have been defeated. Can we see why unity is so very important? Do we really want the world and Satan to see us as defeated? I say "No!"

There are bound to be disagreements from time to time, but we need to deal with them appropriately. Just as in the club, the way to handle disagreements is among our own. The Bible has clear ways to deal with disunity. The first thing is to get our hearts right. Let us be wronged and mistreated, instead of fighting for our rights. We need to deal with the problems internally, not trying to change the circumstance, but allowing God to change our hearts.

The passage above also says to appoint judges to reside over the problem. Other passages say that we should take the person to the Elders of the church and if that will not work, take it to the church. But never are we instructed to take it outside the church. What kind of image is the Church sending when the scandals and problems among church members are published in the newspapers and aired on the television for all the world to see?

In Psalm 133 we read that true unity is like precious oil being poured out and running over the whole body, and there the Lord bestows His blessings. Not only is there strength in unity but there is life as well as God's blessing. Even Jesus prayed for the Church to be unified. In John 17:23 we read, "… that they may be brought to *complete unity*. Then the world will know that you sent me and have loved them even as you have loved me." What a powerful message for the church today! When we are in unity, it makes a statement to the world that Jesus was truly sent from God, and God loves us in the same way He loves Jesus.

The church needs to make it known that if you take on one of us, you have to take on all of us. "One on all and all on one." Not only are you going to have to deal with the whole church, but you have to deal with the Father as well.

We have the Bible and the Holy Spirit as our Enforcer, to help keep us in line with God and His kingdom. So there should be no disunity among us. Why then are there fights and quarrels among believers? The answer is found in James 4:1–5. Fights and quarrels come when we want something and don't get it. This is because we have *become friends* with the world, and *want to consume it on our own lust*. We want the things the world has so much that we are willing to compromise who we are and what we as Christians should stand for. Therefore we are willing to cast aside one of the most powerful forces in the universe—unity.

This is all done to gain something of the world, and in the process, we lose everything. God has not called His church to be defeated, but to be the head and not the tail, to be above and not beneath. We must hold firm to His standard and maintain His unity.

Just like the club we know that without unity we are doomed to defeat. But with it, the gates of hell cannot prevail against us.

CHAPTER FOUR
DISCIPLESHIP
The Prospect

"Therefore go and make disciples of all nations ..."
—Matthew 28:19

In the club we had people who would hang around us just to party, maybe so they could brag to their friends that they were able to do so. As such an exclusive group, not many were invited to hang around us. The few who we did allow to hang around were watched carefully, as possible prospects. In order to hang with us, one had to have been invited by a patch holder (full member), and anyone not invited was made to leave. After hanging around for a while we got to know their character, dependability, and where their loyalties might be, and if we felt they were fit for the chub, we would ask them to be a prospect.

A full member would volunteer to be his sponsor and would become responsible for watching over his prospect. The sponsor would make sure the prospect knew the club rules and what the club expected of him. If the prospect messed up, the patch holder would also have to answer to the club for the prospect. Even though it was the club sponsor who was mainly held accountable for the prospect, everyone in the club would watch him and do all they could to make sure that he would learn the right lessons and work hard to measure up to our standards.

The prospect would attend as many club functions as possible, and considering the rule about not making excuses, you can guess how many club functions were expected of him. The time a person would spend as a prospect was determined on an individual basis. Some prospects learned and grew in club knowledge faster than others. But it could be anywhere from six months to a year for each individual.

While giving the great commission, Jesus tells His disciples to make disciples: "… teaching them to obey everything I have commanded you." Matthew 28:20. This is truly discipleship. In the club, without knowing what it was called, we were making disciples. Granted, they were disciples to the outlaw lifestyle but nevertheless, disciples. Jesus wants Christians to do exactly as the club did. "Go," let me say that again, "Go… and MAKE disciples." Making disciples requires us to spend our time to teach and train people to become disciples.

How does a person find someone to disciple? Let me take a shot in the dark at this. We could invite people to some church functions like potluck dinners, church plays, Christmas programs and many other things that might be going on where Christians hang out.

Just as in the club, a member would invite people to hang with us. You too could invite people to hang with you. Remember the goal of inviting others to club functions was to look for potential future club members. That should be our goal as well for the Church—to increase membership in God's family, the church.

Some will not come. Not everyone invited to club functions came. It was too scary for some, and of no interest to others. Remember what the Word says in Matthew 22:14, "For many are invited, but few are chosen." It is not our job to do the choosing, but to do the calling.

After finding someone who would possibly make a good club member, a sponsor would take him under his wing and train him. That meant spending lots of time with that prospect and helping him in any way he could. The Scripture says to us in 1 Corinthians 4:2 "Now it is required that those who have been given a trust must prove faithful." We have been given a trust to go and make disciples. The Lord Himself has sent us and given us the authority.

I realize that this takes our time and effort, but we need to remember that this is not our time, but God's time. Acts 17:28 says, "For in him we live and move and have our being." We have nothing in this life without God. We cannot even take our next breath without Him. It is for His purpose that we live, not our own. We have been purchased for His purpose. I think the Church may sometimes forget that the purpose is to win a lost world to Christ.

We do not have to commit to train everyone to become disciples, just those who the Lord chooses for us individually. The Bible says in 2 Timothy 2:2 "And the things you have heard me say in the presence of many witnesses entrust to reliable people who will also be qualified to teach others." We do have an obligation to teach and train others to become disciples, but we also must be good stewards of the gift of God. As in the club, let us keep our eyes open for prospective Christians.

Maybe you need somebody to teach you. You may never have been trained yourself. The Church has been lacking in its training and knowledge of what it means to be a disciple making body for Christ. Do not hesitate to ask your pastor or fellow Christians for help. Better to get help than to miss the mark. You may be a prospective member of the body of Christ. Maybe you are one of those people who have been hanging around, but now you feel like you would like to make a commitment to live life no longer as a spectator, but as a patch holder, so to speak. That is what the Church is there for. It is there to help one another grow in the ways of God.

It was not only the sponsor who was responsible for the prospect to learn the ways of the club, and grow to become a full-blown Patch holding member. Every member of the club had an obligation to help prospective members by investing their time, energy, and knowledge to train them in the ways of the club. This was done so we would not lose members, and also that the club looked good to outsiders. We were all on the same page, and nobody did his own thing.

It is important that the Church provide its members with the proper leadership and training so as to advance the kingdom of God. Many times we get busy about things that will have no affect on eternity. In Luke 10:38–42 we read about when Jesus came to the home of Martha during the time of the Feast of Tabernacles, and there were a lot of preparations that had to be done. Martha was busy getting things ready, and in her running around, she was distracted from the teachings of Jesus. Her sister, Mary, was sitting at the feet of Jesus listening to his teachings. Martha got a little upset with her and began to complain.

She came to Jesus and said in verse 40, "Lord do you not care that my sister has left me to serve alone?" So often we focus on things that may need to be done, and in the process, crowd out the important things. The next thing we find ourselves doing is the very thing Martha did. We complain that we don't have enough help, and we tell Jesus what to do to make our lives better. And because we get so loaded down trying to get things done, we think the Lord doesn't care.

Jesus answered Martha in verse 41 and 42, "Martha, Martha, you are worried and troubled about many things. But one thing is needed, and Mary has chosen that good part, which will not be taken away from her." The thing that Mary chose was the one thing the Church needs to choose. We need to sit at the feet of Jesus and quietly listen to the things He has to say. It does not matter what we want to do, what matters most is what Jesus is saying.

Yes, we as individuals need to make disciples. Yes, we as a Church need to make disciples. If an outlaw motorcycle club can figure out that the way to expand and take over territory is to spend their time and resources on growing, knowing that without growth, they will not last, how much more important for God's Church to realize the same and take the necessary steps? If faithful in doing our part, God's Spirit will help us grow and take territory from the evil one. We must learn this lesson—"I must work the works of Him who sent me while it is day; the night is coming when no one can work."

CHAPTER FIVE
BROTHERHOOD
What Is Mine Is Yours, What Is Yours Is Mine

"If anyone has material possessions and sees a brother or sister in need but has no pity on them, how can the love of God be in that person?"
—1 John 3:17

The thing that stands out to me the most from my time as an outlaw biker was the way we treated each other. We were a family, and the bond of brotherhood was the greatest thing we shared. We were close, and everybody watched out for everybody else, whether a prospect or a full patch holder. We had one another's back no matter what.

If the club was out and somebody in the crowd started a fight with a member, the whole club would join in. All of a sudden that person wasn't just fighting one man, they were fighting the whole club. That sent the message to everyone around not to mess with anyone in your club or they could get severely injured. But also, if there was only one club member at a place and something started, the member was not to back away from anyone no matter how many were against him. If he did back down because he was alone and the club found out, *they* would give him a beating. This was so that no matter what, the club did not look like it was afraid. Remember each member was a representative of the club at all times, whether as a group or alone.

Being part of that brotherhood of bikers also meant that no matter where a member went, or what he may get into, there was always, and I mean always, someone he could count on to help. If his bike broke down, he needed money, or bike parts, or maybe just a place to stay, it would be taken care of by one or more of the club members. I remember one time the transmission went out in my car while I was in the area of another chapter of our club, and it was a long way from my home. The club made sure I got home, and by the time I came back to that chapter, they had my transmission replaced and the car ready to go free of charge. We would all do the same for each other. If a brother needed money (even for bail), his brothers had him covered. If someone needed bike parts, we all shared the burden. It was our love of the club and motorcycles that prompted us to act in such a way.

In the book of Acts we read about the early church. It was a real brotherhood. After all, Jesus called us brothers, so they, through the love of Christ, shared their possessions. So in the church it should be the love of Christ and His kingdom that motivates us to have all things in common, and share everything we have, just as the club members' love for the club motivated them to do the same. Acts 4:32–35 is one of the best examples of Christian brotherhood. It says, "All the believers were one in heart and mind. No one claimed that any of their possessions was their own, but they shared everything they had. With great power the apostles continued to testify to the resurrection of the Lord Jesus. And God's grace was so powerfully at work in them all that there were no needy persons among them. For from time to time those who owned land or houses sold them, brought the money from the sales and put it at the apostles' feet, and it was distributed to anyone who had need." Wow, what a concept! These men were *almost* acting like bikers. I said almost. In reality, they were acting better.

Just a side note here for my personal enjoyment—I think James and John, the sons of Zebedee, could have been bikers. After all, Jesus called them "Sons of Thunder." Okay, back to work here—The early Church set the example for us to follow. I don't know where we got off track, but this is the right way to treat one another. I think as a Church, we have gotten caught up in what I call "Get all you can, can all you get, and sit on the lid so no one else gets any." We can preach all we want about brotherhood, but until we start living it, we will miss the boat. Just think how fast our churches would grow if it's members did more giving, rather than using people for gain. There are many who believe that all the church wants is your money. When people would rather go to the bar, or anywhere else but be in church, the church is getting a bad rap, or it's getting what it has earned. Either way, we need to change. We need to promote a true spirit of brotherhood.

People are hurting in the world today and the church needs to lead them to the physician. We must reach out and meet the needs of a struggling world. In Acts 4:33 the Bible says that when the early church acted in this way the apostles were able to testify to the resurrection with GREAT POWER and there was MUCH GRACE upon them ALL. The Church needs that power in our testimony and grace on all we do.

Let us look back at 1 John 3:16–19: "This is how we know what love is: Jesus Christ laid down his life for us. And we ought to lay down our lives for our brothers and sisters. If anyone has material possessions and sees a brother or sister in need but has no pity on them, how can the love of God be in that person? Dear children, let us not love with words or speech but with actions and in truth. This is how we know that we belong to the truth and how we set our hearts at rest in his presence." We, the church, cannot just talk about brotherhood, but we also must live it. It will not be easy; it will take faith. Then remember that faith without works is dead. I fully believe the words of Jesus in Matthew 16, that He will build his church, and the gates of hell will not overcome it. God is calling His Church to "Wake up, sleeper … and Christ will shine on you." Ephesians 5:14. Let us not lose our first love, but remember where we came from, repent, and do the works we did at first.

I want to close this chapter with a few words of encouragement from the books of 1st and 2nd Corinthians. 1 Corinthians 16:13, 14 says, "Be on your guard; stand firm in the faith; be courageous; be strong. Do everything in love." What powerful words for a brotherhood! When God tells us to be on guard, be strong men of courage, firm in faith, and to do everything in love, He is giving us the best mission statement that any church could adopt. If we stay focused on these things, brotherhood will again be strong in the Church. Love never fails. What we did as bikers worked for us. How much more would it work for the people of God!

Let us now look at 2 Corinthians 8:21—"For we are taking pains to do what is right, not only in the eyes of the Lord but also in the eyes of man." As the Church, we can never forget that not only is God watching, but men also are watching to see how we act as a Church, as a body of what we like to call believers. Do we really believe what the Bible says? If so, let us act like it, because there is always somebody watching. There may be someone who has a desire to belong to a family, a brotherhood. Will they, who may be watching how we live want to join the Church, or would they be more likely to find a brotherhood in a bike club? What they see in us as believers will help them decide where they spend eternity.

CHAPTER SIX
OUTREACH
Mandatory Runs

*"...whatever you did for one of the least of these
brothers and sisters of mine, you did for me."*
—Matthew 25:40

Being part of a motorcycle club, there was never a shortage of things to do—parties, runs, and a never-ending series of visiting club members. Most of the time these visits would be just for the sake of being around other club members. You know, the kind of visit you would have on a Sunday as a child, where you would visit your grandmother's house for dinner. I know this sounds funny comparing a visit to grandmother's, to a visit to a fellow biker's house, but we looked forward to visiting, and getting visits from each other in the same way as that eagerness to go to grandmother's, that we felt as children. The Club was truly our family, and spending time with one another was great. There were party runs, party get-togethers, party celebrations, funeral parties, and party parties, but there was also a serious side to what we did. Throughout the year there was a number of what we called *mandatory runs*. These were events that the mother chapter (main chapter over all the other chapters) would set up and every chapter put them on the club calendar. These events were scheduled a year in advance, so there would be no excuse to miss them. They were mandatory, and unlike party runs, could not be missed.

Let me list some of the things that would be considered mandatory. Prison runs, hospital runs, and grave runs. A prison run was when we would go to visit club members who had been incarcerated for various reasons. A hospital run would be to visit members who were in the hospital. And a grave run was when a brother who had died was not forgotten. Usually on Memorial Day, the club would make runs to grave sites and pay tribute to fallen brothers.

Now guess what I found in scripture after I got saved—Matthew 25:31–46. Amazingly, when I read this passage I found that what I was doing as a biker was what I was supposed to be doing as a Christian. Sometimes it blows my mind when I see how God Almighty was preparing me for the Christian lifestyle even while I was a heathen. Matthew 25:31–33 tells us that there will be a day when Jesus will separate the people one from another as a shepherd separates the sheep from the goats. The deciding factor in this account is what we've done for other people. Amazingly, it is not how much we've prayed, or how much money we've given, or not even how many Church services we've attended, but it is how we've reached out to help others. Yes, our outreach is what matters most to the Lord. In verse 35, 36 He says, "For I was hungry and *you gave me* something to eat, I was thirsty and *you gave me* something to drink, I was a stranger and *you invited me* in, I needed clothes and *you clothed me*, I was sick and *you looked after me*, I was in prison and *you came to visit me*." After this, the righteous ask Him when they did this for Him. It was such a part of their lives that they did not even consider it. But Jesus did. Because when they did it for the least of His brothers, they were doing it for Him. If we as the Church really would grasp the powerful message that Jesus is giving us in these passages, we would fall on our faces in fear and trembling. Think about how many times we may have come up with reasons not to visit people in hospitals or prisons—even reasons not to visit our own brothers and sisters in the Lord, when they were in need of spiritual encouragement. And what have we done for the hungry and poor?

Many Christians today think that it's the pastors job to do the visiting. After all, that's what we pay them for. Unfortunately, even many pastors think those kinds of things are beneath them—wait a minute, that is outreach! The Church is supposed to be doing outreach! Who is the church? Is not it the body of believers? It is something that should be so much a part of our daily lives that we do not even realize we are doing it. Both pastors and people alike, who want to call themselves Christians should be doing outreach.

Here we go again: a group of people who have committed their lives to motorcycles and lawlessness are doing the very things that Jesus said that we as Christians should be doing. What is wrong with this picture? The very premise of these passages in Matthew is the separation of sheep and goats. So let's look at the rewards and the consequences. First in verse 41 "Then he will say to those on his left, 'Depart from me, you who are cursed, into the eternal fire prepared for the devil and his angels.'"

I do not believe that there is one person who ever wants to hear those words. The very, very sad thing is that there are some who will indeed hear them. Who are the ones who will hear them? The very people who do not think it is their responsibility to go to the prisons and hospitals, the people who do not think it their place to feed the hungry, the people who do not think that God would ever expect them to help the poor and needy. I am not talking about the lost sinners in this case.

God never expects the sinner to do what is right, He expects it from those who profess to be His children.

I would also like to mention concerning this verse that Jesus said "Depart from me you who are **cursed**." Maybe one of the reasons that so many Christians are struggling in their lives is that they are living under a curse. When I say curse, I'm not talking about some voodoo thing, but a place where it is hard for God to pour out His blessings on their lives. I'm not sure; just some food for thought.

As Christians, we say that we believe the Bible is God's Word for us. One thing I am sure is that we do not get to pick and choose the parts of it that we decide to live by. Either it is God's Word as a whole, or it is not God's Word at all. It tells us how we must live, what we can and cannot do, and that God is not a man that He should lie. Every word is truth. God is truth. There is an old saying—"God said it, I believe it, and that settles it." Pastor Terry Tomlinson, a very good friend of mine, takes this concept further, and says, "God said it, and that settles it, whether I believe it or not." That is a very basic belief that we as Christians need to know—that if God said it, it will happen no matter what we believe about it.

Now that we have looked at the consequences for not reaching out to others, let's look at the rewards for doing good to others. The Lord in verse 46 says, "Then they will go away to eternal punishment, but the righteous to eternal life." Our main goal as Christians is to have eternal life, to live forever with God himself, and His son, Jesus. I do not know about you, but if there is anything I could do to make sure that this would happen for me, I want to do it. When God himself gives us direct insight and knowledge on how to make living with Him and Jesus happen, should we not take it seriously? Take it to heart. Obey his Word. There's nothing confusing here. Jesus made it very clear and easy to understand. Take the life He has given you and use it to touch somebody else, no matter how small the deed is. It never goes unnoticed by God.

Something so small as giving a thirsty person a drink has great rewards from the King of the Universe. The next time you find yourself reasoning in your mind, or making excuses as to why you could never do this or that to help another person, let me tell you about a young couple in a small western Pennsylvania town. It was a number of years ago when I was with a rather large group of bikers. We went to a small town in Pennsylvania called Clearfield. This was not a mandatory run but a party run, There were about fifty to sixty of us and we were at a little bar downtown. There was a lot of noise, a lot of carrying on, and the sound of bike engines roaring.

While I was out on the sidewalk, this young couple probably nineteen to twenty-one years old came walking down the street toward us. There were probably ten or fifteen of us outside, and the door was open to the bar so you could see others and hear the noise quite well. I watched them as they approached, and I could tell that they were scared half to death, but they kept coming and when they got to me they came up and asked if they could give me something. As the young girl held out her hand, I looked down and she had some kind of paper. I was impressed that even though they were so scared, they still came down to where we were, so, I said "Sure." As I took it and looked at it, I saw that it was some kind of religious tract. I thanked them, and they *quickly* walked back the way they came. No, I did not give my life over to Jesus that night, I took the tract home and threw it on the dresser, but this was the beginning of God doing something in my life.

The reason I share this story is so you can see that though the young couple was scared, they still did what they believed God wanted them to do. They may never know, at least in this life, what an impact their little act of faith, combined with the great God they serve had on my life. I will never forget their bravery. That is what got me. I was so impressed with their brave action, and overcoming their fear to bring me the tract that I could not say no.

What is the little thing that God may want you to do? What does God ask us all to do? It is outreach. Nothing is ever so small that God cannot use. It is outreach. I cannot say it enough. Why? Because the church does not do it enough. Oh, how we could change the world and our churches if we would live in such a way as to touch one person each and every day.

In the book of Mark and chapter 9 starting in verse 40 "For whoever is not against us is for us." Verse 41 "I tell you the truth, anyone who gives you a cup of water in my name because you belong to Christ will certainly not lose his reward." There are rewards for outreach—rewards for both you and for the lives you touch. There are rewards now, and throughout eternity. Outreach is not a party but it is a **mandatory run** for the Church.

CHAPTER SEVEN
CHURCH
Club Meetings

"What business is it of mine to judge those outside the church?"
—1 Corinthians 5:12

It never ceases to amaze me the many things that I have found being part of an outlaw motorcycle club that pertain to our Christian walk. I am sure that many of life's situations are the same. In other words, most of us could relate our life experiences to things that God has said should be done as Christians. Just think about your job or past endeavors and how they might relate to a Christian lifestyle. God is always trying to get our attention in order to teach us about His ways. Most of the time, though, we are too busy doing our own thing, that we miss the messages.

In the club, we had weekly meetings. These meetings were called "church." Almost every motorcycle club calls their club meetings "church." Church meetings are different than runs or other club functions. The reason is that what takes place at "church" is totally different from what goes on at any other club function.

Church is where only members are allowed in order for the club business and things pertaining to the club members to be discussed without any disturbance or distraction from outside influence. When "church" is in session the things that take place there are for members' eyes and ears only. No prospects or citizens (non-bikers) are permitted. Members of the club from other chapters are welcome. There are many reasons for this. Among them was the fact that if we were planning or discussing an activity that might be, shall we say, not altogether on the up and up, we knew the people who were there could be trusted. Also it was the time when problems with members could be taken care of..First, we would make sure that everyone was there, and if someone was absent, we would establish whether they let someone know the reason for their absence. Then club business would be discussed. Anything that was causing a problem among the members was taken care of. This was also the time when members paid their club dues. Each member was responsible to make sure their dues were paid or they would lose a portion of their patch. During "church," the club didn't concern itself with what citizens were doing, only what the club members were doing. The main concern was how the members lived. We were to live as 1% bikers at all times. That meant that each member should reflect the values of the club at all times. I will discuss in the next chapter what a 1% biker is. These were the issues that were dealt with at "church."

Let's look at how the "church" meetings in the club compare with our Christian church meetings. In Matthew 13:24–43 Jesus told a parable of the wheat and the weeds growing together. In the parable, an enemy has sown weeds in the field with the wheat. He says to allow them to grow together or by pulling the weeds, the good wheat may be rooted up as well. Jesus said that at the end of the age He will do the weeding and will destroy everything that causes sin and all who do evil. Until this time we have to allow the Holy Spirit to make us holy and live in such a way as not to hinder the working of God in our lives and in our church services.

I know that in our Christian church services we often have believers and non believers in the congregation. How much harder this is, then, to have the presence of God in our church services. Though it is hard, it is not impossible. I say this because all things are possible with God. The scripture is pretty clear in 2 Corinthians 6:17, that we are to come out from among them and be separate. What I am about to say may seem like a strange concept. However, believers and unbelievers should not worship God together. What I am saying is that in a perfect world, and when everything is all said and done, at the conclusion of God's plan this is how it will be. But in the here and now it will not be possible. The reason being that sin has affected everything, even our ability to worship God without outside interference.

I'm sure that some of you are shaking your heads right now and saying, "This guy has lost his mind. How would the church ever grow if we did that?" Some are also saying we need to get them in to the Church so they may become saved. Maybe I can shed a little light on this. The Church is the body of believers—the body of Christ. Shall we look at 2 Corinthians 6:14–18 and see what scripture says. In verse 14 it says, *"Do not be yoked together with unbelievers. For what do righteousness and wickedness have in common? Or what fellowship can light have with darkness?"* We have used this verse many times to tell people they should not marry unbelievers. This is a fine application, but that is not what Paul is talking about here. He is talking about when the Church comes together in their meetings.

When they yoke oxen or horses together, it is so they can pull a plow, wagon, or some other equipment which makes the job get done faster. You would never yoke an ox with a horse. It just will not work. Nothing would ever get done. The ox and horse are two very different animals and cannot work together. So it is with the church. The believer and the unbeliever are two very different types of people. We, as Christians, the Bible says are a new species of being. *We are different.* We have nothing in common with the unbeliever. The verse also says that light can have no *fellowship* with darkness. We are *the light* of the world. How then is it possible to think we can fellowship with the unbeliever, who the Bible says is in darkness? Is it any wonder that the Church has such a struggle for survival? Not only is survival of the Church a concern, but the fact that we come together to worship God and have His presence in our lives to help us change and grow.

Many times, as Christians we leave our Church meetings feeling worse than when we came in. Why? Could it be that the power and presence of God was not among us? Is it possible that the reason for that is that believers and unbelievers mixed together are hindering the working of God's Spirit? I know this sounds tough, but it is important for the Church to be holy as He is holy. That means the individual, as well as the local body of believers must keep themselves from influences that will affect them. Paul says in 1 Corinthians 5:6, "Don't you know that a little yeast leavens the whole batch of dough." In other words, the unbeliever will have an effect on the church as a whole when they meet together.

Some might say that even though there are believers and unbelievers together in our Church services, they feel the presence of God. Many times we mistake our emotional high for the presence of God. When we feel good, we assume it was God. Maybe the music moved us, the preacher's charisma, or some other factor touched our emotions. Always remember that when God shows up, lives are changed forever. When it is an emotion, it only lasts until our mood or circumstances change.

God did great things among the early Church. His power and presence were so strong that the book of Acts 5:13 records that no one else dared join them even though they were highly regarded by the people. With the people highly regarded and God doing great things, verse 14 tells us that more and more men and women *believed* in the Lord and were added to their number. What a powerful verse. The Church was growing because they were keeping themselves pure from outside influence. "Therefore, 'Come out from among them and be separate, says the Lord. Touch no unclean thing and I will receive you.'" 2 Corinthians 6:17. The thing that made the club strong is the same thing that will make the Church strong. Being separate from everybody else when it comes to Church.

Now when it comes to the world, just as the club was not concerned with how the citizens (non-bikers) lived, we also should not judge how the world lives. Do not misunderstand me. I am not saying that we should not be concerned with their salvation. According to 1 Corinthians 5:9–13, we should only judge ourselves as Christians and not those who are unbelievers. Paul says to make sure that we are not having fellowship with those who continue to sin and profess to be brothers in the Lord. But those outside the Church should be judged only by God.

How is this all supposed to work? We, as believers, are to go into the world and preach the gospel. Then those who accept the gospel and believe, we disciple and bring them into the church, and the power of God helps them grow. The church becomes their family, the bond becomes so strong that they want to live in such a way that is pleasing to God, and brings honor to his Church. This is not a new concept, but a much forgotten one. Can you imagine the strength and influence that the church could have in each community if only we would do this? How the lives of Church members would be changed when God moves, heals, and delivers them from their infirmities?

Okay, now what about the club members who were not at church? Well, one thing a club member did was to make sure someone knew they were not going to be there and why. I am sure you may know where I am going with this. You may be thinking *I don't need to tell the church if I am not coming. If I am there, I am there. They don't run my life.* You would be right that the Church does not run your life. God should be the one who runs your life. His Word should be the deciding factor on how you live your life.

So let us see what the Bible says concerning our commitment to the Church. In Hebrews 10:24, 25 we read, "And let us consider how we may spur one another on toward love and good deeds, not giving up meeting together, as some are in the habit of doing, but encouraging one another—and all the more as you see the Day approaching." A few things we learn from this passage are that we can get into a habit of not going to church. One of the reasons we attend Church is to encourage one another. How sad, when we, as the children of God, do not realize our own importance. God himself has chosen us to be His ambassadors here on earth. Just think, the day that you decide not to go to church without a reason might be the day someone needed your words of encouragement. If we believe we are living in the last days, how much more important is it for us to assemble with fellow believers. Times are tough for many today in many ways. If we are not going to be at Church, letting someone know, is not only the right thing, it is the respectable thing to do. Also, when the Church knows the reason you are not going to be there, whether it is illness a family member or other problems, the church will know how they can pray for you. The prayers of the righteous are powerful and effective. When one part of the body hurts, the whole body suffers.

I also want to add that 1 Corinthians 12:12–31 says that the body is a unit made up of many members and each part of the body has a function. The eye has a function, the ear has a function, and so forth. One part cannot say it does not need the other parts. You are a very important part of the body of Christ. When one part of the body is not functioning, the body as a whole suffers.

Not only has God chosen you, He has given you a job that is exclusive to you. So when you come together with the body of believers, you fill a need in that body. And when you are not there, the body is missing a part. 1 Corinthians 12:27 *"Now you are the body of Christ, and each one of you is a part of it."* It is not about the church controlling you, but you taking control of your life for the Church's sake. Remember, Christ loves the church so much He laid down His life for it.

Well now, I get to the hard stuff. I know, you were thinking that was the hard stuff. Sorry, but now I have to discuss the topic of club dues. Yes, the money part. I know that as Christians we are generally givers. In the club it was never a question of paying the dues. We knew there were things that needed to be paid by the club, and we were each glad to give our part. There were regular dues, and then there were the projects that would come up which required us to give more, so we did. The thing I remember most was that we were all proud to be able to help the club in any way we could. Money, time, talents—whatever we had, we were glad to share. Remember the chapter on brotherhood. No one ever complained about the club always needing something.

Why then as Christians do we complain that the church always needs something? As long as there are people to reach, there will always be needs. I hate to say it, but money will be one of those things always needed. I am not going to get into the discussion on whether tithing is still expected of us from God. All I am going to say is, "God so loved the world that He gave." If we love God and are born of Him, then we should be giving also. We give not because the preachers ask us to, or because we will feel guilty if we don't, but because it is in our nature to give. I believe that we should tithe because it is a set amount. In the club, dues were a set amount, and it was not up for debate. Club dues were set by the club USA, the president over all the chapters that were in existence. His word was law; in the sense that you respected it, and did not question it.

It is my belief that we as Christians have a USA so to speak, which is God's Law—the Bible. It is not open for questioning, only for obeying. I know there are some areas where the scripture is silent (does not say one way or another), but in these areas, the Holy Spirit working through your conscience should be your guide. Tithing to some is one of those unclear principles. What I want to do is look at a few scriptures and leave it up to your conscience.

In Matthew 23:23, Jesus says to the teachers of the law *"Woe to you, teachers of the law and Pharisees, you hypocrites! You give a tenth of your spices—mint, dill and cumin. But have neglected the more important matters of the law—justice, mercy and faithfulness. You should have practiced the latter, without neglecting the former."* Did you see that? Jesus said you should do the latter *without neglecting the former.* He does not want us to neglect the giving of our tithes.

In the book of Hebrews 7, verses 1-10, the writer talks about Abraham giving a tenth of everything to Melchizedek. Melchizedek means "king of righteousness without beginning or end, without father or mother." It says that like the Son of God, he remains a priest forever.

This account is in the book of Genesis, chapter 14. What the author of Hebrews goes on to say is that Melchizedek collected a tenth from Abraham and also blessed him. So without a doubt, the lesser is blessed by the greater. There is a blessing when we obey the Word of God. I know there has been a lot of bad teaching on giving. There is a real misconception taught by many that giving will make you rich. What I want you to understand is that it only matters what God says, not what some men say. I only hope that in your tithing, you will be faithful to God. If in this area it is still unclear to you what you should do, let your conscience either convict or acquit you. We have all heard the pleas for us to give to certain ministries. They declare they are good soil and you will reap one hundred fold if you send them money. This may help you a bit to decide how and who to give to.

In 2 Corinthians 9:6, Paul again writes to the Church, "Remember this; whoever sows sparingly will also reap sparingly, and whoever sows generously will also reap generously." Most of the time this part is all we hear of this verse, but if we continue to verse 7, it says, *"Each of you should give what you have decided in your heart to give, not reluctantly or under compulsion, for God loves a cheerful giver."* When we are giving, we are never to give because the preacher wants us to, or because pictures are shown of poor, starving children, or because someone begs money for a certain need. That is giving under compulsion—someone is trying to compel you to give. Never give if you are not sure or if you are reluctant to do so. Never!

Let God speak to your heart, decide in your heart, not with your eyes and ears—then God rewards.

Let me tell a little story about a minister who wanted us to send money. He assured us that it was good soil and there would be a good harvest. So my wife and I sent him some money. Sometime later, we had a financial need of our own. So I called the minister whom we had sent the money to, and explained to him that we had a need. I told him that if a farmer plants corn in a certain field, he does not go to another field for the harvest, but back to the same field he had sown his seed in, and since I had sown in his field, I was coming to him for the harvest. The conversation didn't go as I'd expected. We need to be sure when we are giving, it's for God's purpose, motivated in our hearts by God. If the preachers who preach that they are good soil knew we were coming back to them when we had needs, things would be different.

I once called a Television minister who was asking people to send him one-hundred dollars, and if they could, God would give them one-thousand dollars.

I called and asked if they really believed that. The person on the phone assured me that they did. So I asked them to send me the one-hundred dollars and then they could keep the one-thousand dollars in return. They stumbled around for a while trying to make it sound right, then I just hung up.

Church is important to God and it should be important to us as well. Things are not perfect in the church yet, but if we allow the Holy Spirit to work through us, we'll become the best we can, and it will be as God intends. Christ is the head of the church. He is coming back for a church that is without spot or blemish. He gave Himself up for her to make her holy;

cleansing her by the washing with water through the Word. Through the word! We must be people of the Word and love the bride of Christ. More than any biker can love his club and give himself to his church, we are compelled to love the true Church.

CHAPTER EIGHT
THE 1% BIKER
Only a Few

*"But small is the gate and narrow the road
that leads to life, and only a few find it."*
—Matthew 7:14

What is a 1% biker? I have mentioned the 1% biker in previous chapters. Now I will take some time in this chapter to explain the meaning. I will also draw a correlation between what I see as the 1% Christian.

In 1924, the *American Motorcycle Association* (AMA) was founded. Their goal was to promote motorcycle riding in America. They would sanction motorcycle events such as hill climbs, races, and other sports that promoted motorcycles. One of the things they would do is give awards and trophies to event winners and promote riding groups and encourage participation in their sanctioned events. They even gave prizes to the best-dressed clubs.

In 1947, during an event in Hollister, California a motorcycle club named the *Booze Fighters* made headlines in the news with a story of their wild antics and the way they carried on at the event. News reporters had a field day and even exaggerated some things to make the story more alarming to the public. Soon after, there was a movie made about the Hollister event starring Marlon Brando—*The Wild Ones*. The AMA wrote an article after the news about Hollister got out, stating that 99% of all their members were law-abiding citizens and only 1% of the biker communities were "outlaws."

This began what is known as the 1% biker—bikers who are committed to living their way of life. They do not care about what the AMA says, nor about what others think about them. They are rebels-outlaws and are separate from the rest of the biker population.

As far as the best dressed, they decided to wear a three-piece patch that also set them apart. They decided to chop down their bikes and ride hard, drink, and march to the beat of their own drum. Their three-piece patches became known as their colors. It identified their club and where they were from, as well as their club logo.

Outlaw clubs are the only biker clubs that wear a three-piece patch. Plus, they wear a diamond shaped patch with the 1% biker logo in the middle of the diamond. This patch is much smaller and can be worn on their vest. It's typically on the left shoulder or the back. The club they belong to may determine where it should be worn. Some club members may wear a "NOMAD" patch for their bottom rocker. This is when a member lives like a nomad traveling from one club chapter to another with no specific home. He may move around because of weather or many other reasons.

I hope that this helps you to better understand what outlaw clubs are and how they came into existence. There are quite a few bikers and biker cubs, but only a very few that can wear the 1% biker patches. The wearing of the 1% diamond and the three piece patch is earned. A 1% club also must approve it, otherwise, your life is at risk by wearing it. These clubs are very territorial. They are also very proud of who they are and what they stand for. Remember, not everyone can make it as a 1% biker. It is a hard challenge and few make the cut. Remember, it is not something you can halfheartedly decide to do. It is a commitment to the lifestyle as a whole. Being part of a 1% club gives that extra sense of belonging to something special, that one thing that will set you apart from all the other motorcycle clubs.

So here is my thinking about 1% bikers and what I would like to call 1% Christians. I would like to see 1% of the Christian population live in such a way as to separate themselves from the so-called norm of Christian living. I would like to see them dress differently, live differently, act differently. They should be so different than the average Christian today that the world would take notice of them. They should be like the early disciples in the book of Acts.

Acts 4:13 says, "When they saw the courage of Peter and John and realized that they were unschooled, ordinary men, they were astonished and they took note that these men had been with Jesus." Did you get that? That courage they saw in Peter and John is what I am talking about. We need to live as men and women of courage. Believe me when I say that it took courage to be a 1% biker. It is a lifestyle that challenges you to go beyond the average biker. To be a 1% biker meant that one would fight harder, ride harder, and do everything better than the average biker.

That is what we need in the church—Christians who will challenge themselves to fight the ways of the world, the lust of the flesh, and the devil's schemes harder than the average Christian. We need to live better than an average Christian lives. **Do not be average!** I get so excited about this that I can hardly contain myself.

We need to realize that we belong to the most exclusive club in the world. We are picked by God Himself to belong. I have often said that God picked us to live in this time of earth's history. We are the best He has for what needs to be done to spread the gospel in this day and age. If Martin Luther, John Wesley, Charles Spurgeon, John Calvin, or any other great men or women of God could do better than you or I, God would have had them born at this time. He chose us to belong to His family, which is so much greater in my eyes than belonging to a family of bikers.

There are approximately 247 million people in the United States who profess to be Christians, and I know we profess to be a Christian nation. But if we are honest with ourselves, there is something terribly wrong when that many people profess to be Christians and we still have the secular problems we have. What I mean is this, you would think that with 247 million people living for God we would see the crime rate and the number of people suffering from depression much lower, just to mention a couple of the things plaguing our nation.

I do not doubt anyone's Christianity, but what I am saying is that to live according to God's Word is quite a challenge. It's no easy thing. There are no shortcuts that will help to advance the gospel and God's kingdom. However, changing the nation, and even the world, will take much more than what we have been doing. It can be done, but it will take a select few to commit to doing the right thing, the biblical thing, and the godly thing to make it happen.

Remember the early church? There were only a few disciples who turned the world upside down, or right side up, depending on how you look at it. They did it by being committed to the words of Christ. They were twelve ordinary men who, by their refusal to compromise, set in motion events that would have everlasting effects on the world.

Most people do not believe that they can make a difference. What I want you to remember is something somebody once told me. "You and God together make a majority." Remember that the King of the Universe is on your side. God almighty is with you. Romans 8:31, 35–37 says, "What, then, shall we say in response to these things? If God is for us, who can be against us? ... Who shall separate us from the love of Christ? Shall trouble or hardship or persecution or famine or nakedness or danger or sword? As it is written: 'For your sake we face death all day long; we are considered as sheep to be slaughtered.' No, in all these things we are more than conquerors through him who loved us."

What a powerful word from God to us. He is with us. It is not easy; there will be hard times, and it is going to take commitment, but we will win! We can make a change. We can and will win the battles in His strength. I read the end of the Book, and we win. We have to be willing to do whatever God calls us to do.

I know that not many are familiar with the biker world, and that may be a good thing. You have not had to go through that lifestyle. Some reading this book may relate to my old way of life and that also can be a good thing. I still love to ride motorcycles; I love the wind in my face and the feeling of freedom I get, when on my bike. I thank God that He saved me from a lifestyle of riotous living. One thing I am also thankful for is the lessons I learned through my time spent in that lifestyle and what I have been able to apply to my Christian walk.

The 1% biker is, as I said, a different level of motorcycle rider than all other motorcycle riders. Trying not to beat an old horse, but what has set us apart was the level of commitment we had to our lifestyle and our club. Though we were all bikers, 1% bikers lived what we would consider a cut above the rest, and this lifestyle was not only recognized by us, but by the rest of the biker community. They knew we were different and lived according to a higher standard, as biker standards go that is.

This is my challenge to Christians everywhere. Live above the norm of how most would consider a Christian to live. If there are approximately 247 million Christians in the United States, I would like to see 1% of them live in such a way that their lifestyle would be recognized as so different that the Christian community as a whole would be inspired to do the same. Just think, that would be 2.47 million Christians living to have a powerful effect on this nation. That is very few. Though according to the AMA, only 1% of the biker population was considered outlaw, we still see the powerful influence they have had from 1947 until today. Not to give glory to any clubs, but we know some 1% clubs just by their names—*The Hells Angels*, for example. I won't go on naming others, but my point is that we have all heard of them.

I would love in the near future for people to notice that there is a group of Christians, who are shaking the world with their lifestyle and their commitment to spreading the gospel.

I want to tell you about a group of 1%ers in the Bible. They were led by a nobody of their day. He didn't come from a family of importance. He was no great warrior, at least in the world's eyes. There was nothing at that time to make him stand out. His account is recorded in the book of Judges. This man was named Gideon. In Judges chapter 6, we read the account of Gideon. First we should note that the Israelites had done evil in the eyes of God, so He gave them over to the Midianites. For seven years the Midianites would come whenever the Israelites planted their crops and ruin them. They would not spare a living thing. No crops, no cattle, no sheep, not even a donkey was safe from destruction.

Then the Israelites called out to God, and God sent an angel to speak to Gideon. Gideon was hiding in a winepress threshing wheat to keep the Midianites from destroying it. The angel said to Gideon, "The LORD is with you, mighty warrior." Then in Judges 6:13, Gideon, sounding so much like most of us, replies "Pardon me, my lord, … but if the LORD is with us, why has all this happened to us? Where are all his wonders that our ancestors told us about when they said, 'Did not the LORD bring us up out of Egypt?'"

He is basically saying, *"Where are all those miracles I hear other people talking about? I have heard the stories, but I never get to see any miracles in my life."* It is easy to complain when things don't seem to be working in our favor. Sometimes we may be hoping to just get by somehow, and maybe even hiding as Gideon was in the winepress, but God might be asking us to step out.

Then Gideon, like many of us, thinks that the Lord has abandoned him. Do not ever forget Hebrews 13:5,6 "<u>Never</u> will I leave you; <u>never</u> will I forsake you. So we say with confidence, 'The Lord is my helper; I will not be afraid. What can man do to me?'" (emphasis added). God Himself is your help, and He will never abandon you. Do not let your fears get the best of you or keep you from fulfilling God's plan and purpose for your life. Like Gideon, God has greater plans for you than you may know. Gideon thought he was nobody, but God saw greater things in him than he saw for himself. You, my friend, are the same.

I could never have seen myself doing things for God when I was hiding from him in the club. Remember, you are the best God has for this time in history. And God does not make junk. No matter where you may think you're hiding, God knows exactly where you are. As Moses tended sheep in the desert for forty years, God knew exactly where he was, and when God needed him for another purpose, He called him by name. Like Gideon in the winepress, God knows where and who you are, and He has great plans for your future.

God not only knew where Gideon was, but tells him in Judges 6:16 "I will be with you, and you will strike down **_all_** the Midianites" (emphasis added). God told him **_I_** will be with you—but **_you_** will strike down **_all_** the Midianites. Gideon and God are a majority, just like you and God are a majority and cannot be defeated. I am going to skip past the signs Gideon asked for and move on to the choosing of Gideon's help for the battle that is ahead with the Midianites, which we find in Judges 7.

In verse 2 God tells Gideon that he has too many men for him to deliver the Midianites into his hands. God says that if Israel defeats the Midianites, they may boast that her own strength has saved her. God told Gideon to send home anyone who trembles with fear. Out of thirty-two thousand men, only ten thousand remained. God told Gideon that this was still too many men! Sometimes it may seem as if God is setting us up for failure, when He is actually setting us up for victory in a way that makes it clear that He deserves the credit.

Then God says to take the men to the water and separate those who lap with their tongues like a dog from those who get down on their knees and drink. Three hundred men lapped like a dog, and God said that with those three hundred He would save the Israelites and give the Midianites into his hands. So Gideon sent the rest of the Israelites back to their tents.

Gideon takes the three hundred men, divides them into three companies of one hundred men each. He then gives them each a trumpet and an empty jar with torches inside. At Gideon's command, they are to blow their trumpets and smash their jars. *Gideon essentially tells them, "Watch me. Follow my lead, do exactly as I do."* They blew the trumpets and broke the jars. With trumpets in one hand and torches in the other, they shouted "A sword for the LORD and for Gideon." The Midianites ran, crying out as they, fled, and the Lord caused them to turn on each other.

The Midianites were Gideon's enemy whom he had to face. Your enemy might be with the "bill-ites" the "sick-ites" the "neighbor-ites" or any number of "ites" you may be struggling with. Remember do not hide, but seek God. Follow His Word, and you will win. Like Gideon, we all need some help from others from time to time.

Yes, with God's help, Gideon and his men were victorious. This never would have happened, had Gideon and his men not lived and acted differently than the rest of the Israelite nation. Gideon's message to his men was clear: "Watch me; follow my lead." I would that we had more men and women like Gideon who would say "Watch me, follow me, do what I am doing, and you will be all right." Most Christians today say "Don't look at me; keep your eyes on God, not on me. I am human, and I will let you down." This sounds fine and noble, but it is not what the Bible says.

Paul, the apostle, when he writes to the Corinthian church makes this statement in 1 Corinthians 4:16–17 "Therefore I urge you to imitate me. For this reason I am sending to you Timothy, my son whom I love, who is faithful in the Lord. He will remind you of my way of life in Christ Jesus, which agrees with what I teach everywhere in every church." There it is. Paul says to watch how he lives and to imitate his life and Timothy's life, because it will remind you of his life in Christ. Think about it—the only way people are going to see Christ is if they see Him in your life. How you live and how you act should be testifying to the life of Christ. We should all, like Paul and Gideon, be able to show by our actions that we are different from the norm.

Another detail I'd like to focus on regarding God's victory through Gideon and his men is what they had in hand that God was able to use to defeat the enemy. They had a trumpet in one hand and a light in a clay pot in the other. Many times in the Bible, we see trumpets in battle. Joshua marched around the walls of Jericho. He then gave orders to blow the trumpets and shout, and the walls came down. I think one of the things that God is trying to get us to learn is that sometimes you have to make a little noise for the things of God. Too many times the Church just sits quietly while the things of the world take over the things of God. It is time to shout from the rooftops and blow the trumpets in Zion. What I mean to say is that as Christians we need to be more vocal concerning our beliefs. We can no longer afford to sit quietly while the world and the devil pass us by. They are not only passing us by, but they are doing their best to silence us. God's Word says in 2 Timothy 1:7 "For the Spirit God gave us does not make us timid, but gives us power, love and self-discipline."

Also, we should be able to let our light shine from the earthen vessels. The hardest thing is to allow our vessels to be broken so the light may shine forth. Second Corinthians 4:6–7 reads "For God, who said, 'Let light shine out of darkness,' made his light shine in our hearts to give us the light of the knowledge of God's glory displayed in the face of Christ. But we have this treasure in jars of clay to show that this all-surpassing power is from God and not from us." The power is from God, it is not our own. We, like Gideon and many others, must trust God's Word and God's power in us. We, as Christians, should be prepared for battle. We have the weapons of warfare, but they are spiritual and not carnal, and they are mighty to bring down strongholds.

Finally, I want to focus our attention on Gideon's men. Remember, he started out with 32,000 men, then God had him send 22,000 who trembled in fear back to Mount Gilead. God then had him send another 9,700 who drank while on their knees, leaving only 300 men who would follow him and be victorious over the Midianites. 300 from 32000 would be 1% who were left. Now tell me that does not want to make you shout.

I tell you that if we as Christians could just decide that we want to be in the 1% of the Christian population, that we want to go beyond the norm, and live in such a way that others see and are challenged to do the same, God can use us and do great things through us. The Church today needs men and women who will take the challenge, step up and live godlier than they have ever lived, study the Word harder than they have ever studied, pray more than they have ever prayed, give more of themselves than ever, love more than ever, serve more, allow Christ to fully take us over. 1% is not a _big_ number at all, but it could make a _big_ impact on our nation and the Church. Think about it, pray about it.

Decide in your heart that you will be part of the 1% that will be ready when God calls. Decide not to be afraid, not hiding, but willing to come out from among them and be separate. And let God live through you. Are you willing to say, as said in Isaiah 6:8 "Then I heard the voice of the Lord saying, Whom shall I send? And who will go for us? And I said, Here am I. Send me!"

CHAPTER NINE
IF BIKERS CAN DO THIS,
WHY CAN'T WE?
What Are We Afraid Of?

"He said in a loud voice, 'Fear God and give him glory, because the hour of his judgment has come. Worship him who made the heavens, the earth, the sea and the springs of water.'"
—Revelation 14:7

Before I joined the 1% club, as I said earlier, I sat down and counted the cost. That cost being what I would have to give up, what I would have to change, and also what I would be gaining by joining such an organization. After careful thought, my mind was made up: *yes, I wanted to join.* My thoughts were not so much about what I would be giving up, as they were about what I would be gaining.

I think this is the way most of us make our decisions—not based on what we might lose, but on what we will gain. For instance, if we want to buy something new, say a car or something else, we may give some thought to the price. We might consider payments, or we may think about the condition of our current car. Often when people think about a new item, they think about how nice it will look (or how good we will look in it).

My main thought about joining the biker club, the 1% club, was that I was doing something that not everyone could do even if they wanted to. Some may try to join, but not be accepted. Many others would just decide that it would be too hard for them. Others would not want someone or something controlling their lives, telling them what to do or where to be at certain times or for certain reasons.

Not me! I knew I could do it. I am a person of determination. Once I make up my mind, there is nothing I cannot do. (By the way, this is not always a good thing). What I was gaining was respect or fear. I knew I was getting one or the other from most of the people that I met. Soon my motto became "respect or fear," and that was my goal at the time. It seemed to work well until God got ahold of me, that is. I later realized that the reason it worked with the club was that they demanded people to either respect who they were or they would soon learn what it was to fear them.

This is not only true with outsiders (non-club members), but also within the ranks of the club. One of the reasons that members attended runs, parties, or club meetings was that they had respect for them or the reason for the events. The other reason was they feared what would happen if they did not attend such events. I mentioned in earlier chapters how one could be fined for not showing up to meetings, or a piece of his colors, or even the whole set of colors may be taken from him. This meant loss of authority or even rank in the club, and nobody wanted that. They also could, or should I say would, be beaten severely for noncompliance. The severity of the beating would depend on the infraction or the number of times you had to be disciplined. Some could even be beaten and thrown out of the club. You may think that it would be a good thing to be thrown out. But if you were thrown out, you would also lose your bike and probably any other property you had at the time. Plus, for an added bonus, anytime club members would see you after that you'd get another beating.

How, you might wonder does this have anything to do with our relationship with God? I would like to give you a few of my thoughts on these things, and share what the Bible says concerning them. I believe that many people who make a decision to follow God, do so based mostly on what they are going to receive rather than on what they may have to give up or change. What I mean is that many look forward to the fact that they will be spending eternity in heaven. You know—streets of gold, gates of pearls, no sorrow, no more tears, plus God Himself and His Son Jesus there with us. This is all great and all true, but our decision, our commitment to God and His Word and whether we even make it to heaven is based on our actions here and now.

When we accept Jesus as our Savior and Lord, it is based on the fact that we are sinners and cannot save ourselves. We need His help. We need His help so that we can live lives that are clean and pure from sin. Remember, _we are sinners_ because that is what we do— we sin. The book of Romans 3:23 says, "… for all have sinned and fallen short of the glory of God." In order for us to make it to heaven and the pearly gates, we must first trust God's living Word and allow the power of the Holy Spirit to change us. It is not a one-time decision, but a lifestyle that we must live. There is no way for us to live that life without allowing God to continually change us and recreate us into the image of His Son. We can never look ahead at what we might gain without looking at the here and now, and what we have to lose. When I say what we might lose, I mean the sin that trips us up. Let us look at the book of Hebrews.

Hebrews 12:1-7 "Therefore, since we are surrounded by such a great cloud of witnesses, let us throw off everything that hinders and the sin that so easily entangles. And let us run with perseverance the race marked out for us, fixing our eyes on Jesus, the pioneer and perfecter of faith. For the joy set before him he endured the cross, scorning its shame, and sat down at the right hand of the throne of God. Consider him who endured such opposition from sinners, so that you will not grow weary and lose heart. In your struggle against sin, you have not yet resisted to the point of shedding your blood. And have you completely forgotten this word of encouragement that addresses you as a father addresses his son? It says, 'My son, do not make light of the Lord's discipline, and do not lose heart when he rebukes you, because the Lord disciplines the one he loves, and he chastens everyone he accepts as his son.' Endure hardship as discipline; God is treating you as his children. For what children are not disciplined by their father?"

Did you catch that? *Throw off everything that hinders and the sin that easily entangles you.* Also, *look ahead and run with perseverance the course laid out for you.* God has a course that He has laid out for us. We do not get to run any direction that we want. He disciplines us as sons, because He loves us. We often forget about God's discipline and God's plans for us. So many Christians do not even want to hear that God disciplines us. All they want to hear about is God's love, but as we just read, God disciplines those He loves. You cannot separate God's love from His discipline. Though many today may try, the two are inseparable.

I would challenge you to see how many sermons you hear today on God's discipline, the Fear of the Lord, or even Hell for that matter. Those sermons are few and far between. The reason is that they are not popular with the masses. Peace and prosperity is the message for today's churches. It soothes the carnal mind and makes us feel good. But it is not helping Christians one bit; because it's actually causing greater damage to the unbeliever. You may ask *why*? Do you remember why I joined the club? **Fear** and **respect**—and remember that is what I wanted. When there is no discipline, there is no respect, and where there is no discipline, there is no fear.

If a child is not shown discipline, that child will soon have no respect, because they have no fear of consequences. The sad thing about Christians today is that they believe that as children of God there are no consequences for their loose living practices. They are taught that God is love, and with love there is no pain. Even more troubling is the fact that they are taught that if there is some pain in their lives, it is because they do not have enough faith in God.

Let's look at Hebrews 12:9. "Moreover, we have all had human fathers who disciplined us and we **respected** them for it. How much more should we submit to the Father of our spirits and live!" The writer goes on to say that no discipline seems pleasant, but painful. It does, however, produce a harvest of righteousness. I know there are many who would love to get to heaven without allowing the Holy Spirit to change one thing about themselves; but it just will not happen.

Like the club, God also requires two things—respect and fear. Ok, I know the whole discipline thing was hard enough, but that has to do with respect. Remember the King of the Universe is choosing us. He has a plan for us. He has a call upon our lives, a purpose, a destiny for us, but you and I must **respect** the fact that He is God and we are not. He gets to call the shots; and we don't. He wrote the Book; we get to obey it. We need to realize that God not only gave us His Word, but He also gave us His Spirit to dwell in us and change us. He did this so that men everywhere would call on Him. We should respect God because He sent his Son to take our place on the cross and to die for our sins. Because He made this sacrifice, we can be forgiven. Yes he deserves our respect! He is the Almighty, the King of kings.

Once again, I have to say that was not the hard stuff. One final subject I would like to touch on is the fear of God. If you are still reading, praise God you have not given up yet. You may be aiming for that 1%er status. Another sticky subject for many Christians is the fear of God. Why? Because we hear so much about God's love that we think that we have nothing to fear from Him. In our minds, there should be nothing to fear from One who loves us. Before I go on, let me ask you three simple questions. Do you believe that your father and mother love you? I am sure almost everyone has answered yes. Second question: was there ever a time you did something wrong and you were afraid they would find out? If you are honest, you also answered yes to the second question. Third and final question: Why were you afraid? If you are honest, and I believe you are, you were afraid of what they would do when they found out what you had done. Even though you know they love you, you knew there would be consequences. Why then is it so hard for us to believe that God loves us, is our Heavenly Father, yet there should be reason to fear Him? This fear only has to do with wrong doing. When we do right we have nothing to fear, but when we do wrong, fear is there. That fear is to help us to keep doing right. Let me illustrate this in another way. Suppose you are going seventy in a fifty-five mile per hour speed zone. While you do that, you probably fear the police. Why? Because there will be consequences for you violating the law. Violators will be prosecuted. The same is true with God. If you violate God's Law, there are consequences. I know we hardly ever think of it this way, but that is how it works. The consequences are there for you to learn not to break the Law.

Now that I have you thinking about it, I am going to give you some scriptures to help the biblical truth concerning the fear of God come to the forefront of your mind.

Before anyone starts to question the word *fear* and its meaning, let me help you. The Hebrew word used in the Old Testament for fear in most of its passages is "yir'ah." It means "fear, exceedingly fearful, dreadful, reverence." I have heard many times that it does not really mean that we should be afraid of God. However, that is exactly what it means.

The word used in the Greek in the New Testament is "Phobeo." It means "to frighten, to be alarmed, fear exceedingly, awe, or reverence." Shall we see now what Jesus said concerning the fear of God in the book of Luke? Luke 12:4, 5 says, "I tell you, my friends, do not be afraid of those who kill the body and after that can do no more. But I will show you whom you should fear: Fear him who, after the killing of the body, has the power to throw you into hell. Yes, I tell you, fear him." Jesus makes it clear that we are to fear Him who has the power over us even after the body is dead. Only God has that power. Jesus also goes on to tell them how valuable they are and not to be afraid. I know it almost sounds like counter diction, but if we were to look at the passages as a whole, they make sense. Jesus starts out warning them about the yeast, or the hypocrisy of the Pharisees. He says there is nothing hidden or concealed that will not be brought to light. In other words, do not try to hide what you are doing wrong because you will be held accountable in the end if you haven't repented. Confess it, get it out in the open, and let God deal with it. Let God have the opportunity to forgive you and allow His Holy Spirit to change the behavior that is causing you to sin.

When we were children and had done something wrong, it was often our inclination to hide it from our parents. When we did not tell, and they found out another way, we were in a lot more trouble than we would have been, had we told them ourselves! We just had to remember that they loved us, and if we confessed to them, they would help us so, we did not do the same dumb thing over again. That is what Jesus is trying to get us to see. It is the same with God. He loves us and wants us to come to Him for help. Do not hide your sins from Him, but confess to Him so He can forgive and help you. Do not make excuses for your bad behavior. After all, God knows everything we've done before we tell Him. He wants you and I to realize that we are valuable to Him. Like our earthly parents, He expects us to come to Him and tell Him our sins. Nobody likes discipline, but just as our parents told us, *"it's for your own good,"* God wants us to be the very best we can be, and if we let Him correct us, we will be.

Psalm 111:10 says, "The fear of the Lord is the beginning of wisdom; all who follow His precepts have good understanding. To him belongs eternal praise." If the fear of God is the beginning of wisdom, it is no wonder that our nation, as well as most of the Church, is in such trouble. I believe that we have lost the fear of the Lord. As I mentioned above, what God wants from His children is to confess our wrong-doing to Him and allow Him to fix us. Instead, many Christians today want God to see things their way, instead of them seeing things His way. What the Church once viewed as sin, we now view as acceptable! What at one time was wrong is now seen as right, and what was once viewed as righteous and holy has now become unacceptable.

This is nothing new. Isaiah 5:20 puts it this way: "Woe to those who call evil good and good evil, who put darkness for light and light for darkness, who put bitter for sweet and sweet for bitter." Why have we become like this? It is because we want to be accepted by all! We want everybody to like us. We surely do not want people to think we are any different than they are. But we are supposed to be different! I am grieved that the church has compromised so much to the point that it's difficult to distinguish the believer from the unbeliever. It all starts with losing our fear of God. We have become more afraid of what other people think of us than what God thinks of us. We tell ourselves "Oh, it is not that bad, a little compromise is okay. After all, if we do not compromise, the church will not grow." We are afraid that people will not like us because they will think we are too judgmental. They will say, "you Christians are too close minded." We do not want people to reject us. We are afraid of rejection!

Our problem is that we are afraid of the wrong type of rejection. Remember, Jesus said "Do not be afraid of the one who can kill the body, but fear the one that after the body has been killed has the **power** to throw you into hell." Let us concern ourselves with pleasing God, rather than people. Paul wrote to the Galatian Church and warned them about deserting Christ and turning to another gospel, which he warned was no gospel at all. Paul warned about a perverted gospel that was throwing them into confusion. In Galatians 1:10 Paul says, "Am I now trying to win the approval of human beings, or of God? Or am I trying to please people? If I were still trying to please people, I would not be a servant of Christ." Being a people pleaser will only hinder our walk with God and confuse the true gospel.

The club never tried to please people to get them to join or to get others to like them. They had a set of rules and standards that they lived by, no matter what others thought about them. We as Christians should live the same way for God. We should live by His Word and His standard, and never compromise our lifestyle to please others. One thing that I have learned over the years is that anytime you compromise to gain something, you always lose what you gained in the compromise. Just a few more scriptures that will help us understand some of the benefits for having a fear of the Lord. Proverbs 10:27—"The fear of the LORD *adds length to life*, but the years of the wicked are cut short" (emphasis added). I love this! This passage is saying that the fear of God is good; it adds life. How do we know it is good besides adding life? Because he says the wicked have their years cut short. Fearing God is a good thing! Proverbs 15:33—"**Wisdom's instruction [to man]** is to fear the LORD, and humility comes before honor" (emphasis added).

So Fear of the Lord is also a teacher for us. It teaches wisdom. Wisdom is the ability to properly use knowledge. Maybe this could be a part of the problem with the church. If there is no fear of God, then there can be no wisdom to use the Bible knowledge we have. Therefore, we have teachers teaching the Bible in their own understanding. Not being taught by the Holy Spirit, but by themselves or even others who have no fear of God. No fear, and no wisdom! Proverbs 19:23: "The fear of the LORD *leads to life*; Then one rests content, untouched by trouble" (emphasis added).

I believe the writer is talking about life in Christ. In Him we live, and move, and have our being (Acts 17:28). There is no life outside of Christ. John 10:10 says, "… I have come that they may have **life** and have it to the full" (emphasis added). There is no rest without Christ. Matthew 11:28 tells us "Come to me, all you who are weary and burdened, and I will give you

rest" (emphasis added). Contentment comes through Christ. 1 Timothy 6:6 says, "But godliness with **contentment** is great gain" (empahsis added). In Him we are untouched by trouble! Romans 8:35-37 reads "Who shall separate us from the love of Christ? Shall **trouble** or hardship or persecution or famine or nakedness or danger or sword? As it is written: 'For your sake we face death all day long; we are considered as sheep to be slaughtered,' No, in all these things we are more than conquerors through him who loved us" (emphasis added)

These are just a few things we are missing out on by not having a fear of God. I know this is a hard subject to grasp. We, as the people of God, have to take God at His whole Word, not just the parts we like and those that make us feel good. The God of the New Testament is the same God in the Old Testament. He clearly says in the book of Malachi 3:6 "I the LORD do not change." Some think the God of the Old Testament is a God of wrath, and the God of the New Testament is a God of love. He is One. He's the same God, but there are times we will know His love and times we will know His wrath.

One of the main things that kept the club in order and on track was the leadership. The leadership had to be strong and unwavering in the decisions they made. If the leaders had wavered in their decision making, the club would have been ever wavering. Had the leadership been weak, the whole club would have been weak, and would not have lasted against our enemies. Strong leadership is the key to success in any enterprise. Whether it is a secular or Christian organization; as the leadership goes, so goes the organization. When we have a Church that has lost the fear of the Lord and has lost respect, it means we need leaders who will stand up to teach and preach these powerful truths. I do not mean just pastors and preachers, though they are needed. I mean, as Christians, we need to take a stand and proclaim these biblical truths. Again if only 1% of the Christians in the United States would grab the reigns and speak out, the Church can and will change, I believe that God Almighty will bless the work of their hands and will move in such a way as to shine the light of Truth on them as His Word is being proclaimed.

God's Word is full of accounts about His people falling away and then being restored. In these accounts, God always raises up a person or people to lead them. Moses, Abraham, Joshua, David, and Samson are just a few of the many. God always uses ordinary people to accomplish extraordinary feats for Him.

When we read the book of Judges, we can see a pattern that developed with the Israelites. After Joshua and his whole generation died, another generation grew up who did not know the Lord or what He had done for them. Then they did evil in God's eyes and served and worshiped all kinds of false gods. But God, in His mercy, would raise to leadership a judge for them. Whenever God would raise a judge to lead them in His Word, the Israelites would serve God. However when the judge would die, they went back to their evil ways. Leadership is very important.

The book of Hosea summarizes what I am trying to say. In Hosea 4:5–9 we read "You stumble day and night, and the prophets stumble with you. So I will destroy your mother— my people are destroyed from lack of knowledge. Because you have rejected knowledge, I also reject you as my priests; because you have ignored the law of your God, I also will ignore your children. The more priests there were, the more they sinned against me; they exchanged their glorious God for something disgraceful. They feed on the sins of my people and relish their wickedness. And it will be: Like people, like priests. I will punish both of them for their ways and repay them for their deeds."

The priests, the leaders of the people, fed on the sins of the people and did nothing to correct them. The priests were increasing in number, and there was no faithfulness to God or love of God. Instead, they were worried about their own positions. The priest wanted to please the people more than they wanted to please God. They even made a profit from the people's sins.

I'm sad to say that it's much like that in the church today. Many pastors and other leaders are making a profit by not confronting sin in church. If a church leader confronts someone about their sin, they may leave, and if they leave, they take their money with them. If they take their money, the church building payment may not get paid, or the pastor's salary might suffer. You see, it becomes easy to please men rather than God. And many times it is done without thinking about it this way. However when the church becomes indebted to the things of the world, we become slaves to those things.

God says He will punish both people and priest alike for their deeds. This is why we as Christians must live above the norm, above the rest of the world and its ways. We need strong, Godly leadership in the church to produce strong, Godly men and women. If we are honest with ourselves as we look around at the church today, we can see things that not long ago, were unacceptable. Some say this is because the church has progressed, but I say it is because the church has compromised God's Word and His commandments for Christian living. There used to be a time when the Church was impacting the world. The world at this time is impacting the church. I believe now is the time to change this. Remember, we can make a difference. We just have to start where we are. Speak out, speak up, and let our voices be heard. The squeaky wheel gets the grease, so to speak. Yes, it is time to make some noise. It is time to shout, blow the trumpets, rev those engines. We need to get going and do something great with God. Someone once made a statement that I really liked. He said, "If you are going to do something, do something so big that if God is not in it, it will fail."

CHAPTER TEN
POSERS
The Great Pretenders

*"Then I will tell them plainly, 'I never knew
you. Away from me, you evildoers!'"*
—Matthew 7:23

One night I was out with some friends at an establishment that was not too far from my home. We were just hanging out, shooting pool, and having a few drinks. I was not flying colors that day. When I say *not flying colors,* this means that I did not have my club colors on. We were just hanging at a biker bar. Many people who ride motorcycles like to hang out together even though they may or may not be club members. They still share a common bond—their love of motorcycles.

On this day, a particular man was there whom I'd never seen before. We were shooting pool and having a conversation. I cannot remember what we were talking about, but somewhere along the line he told me that he was a member of a very infamous 1% outlaw club. He had the bike and clothes and even some of the language. He may have looked like he could have been an outlaw biker, but there was still something missing. Well that peaked my interest, since he did not know I was a member of another 1% club. When I started to ask him some questions that he did not have answers for, I knew he was lying. Now he had just committed the two things that would really make me angry. Number one—he lied to me, and number two—he professed to be something he was not. He pretended to be part of a club whose members give their lives to. Regretfully, his day went from bad to worse.

I am telling you this story because it is a very important lesson for us to realize. There are many people out there who pretend to be something they are not. It is no different in the Christian realm. I have in my lifetime met more than a few people who profess to be Christians, but they do not measure up. What I am saying is they have the Bible, they may go to church and most of the things we would expect from Christians, but there is something missing.

You may be thinking: *Don't judge,* but the Bible says in Matthew 7:15, 16 to "watch out for false prophets. They come to you in sheep's clothing, but inwardly they are ferocious wolves. By their fruit you will recognize them. Do people pick grapes from thorn bushes, or figs from thistles?" In other words, on the outside they look like sheep, but it is what is on the inside of a person that counts. It may be difficult to distinguish at first, but after talking to a person for a while, out of the abundance of the heart the mouth will speak (Luke 6:45).

After talking to the biker at the bar for a few minutes, I knew he was not what he said he was. He may have fooled others, but my firsthand knowledge of the 1% biker world was something he did not count on. As Christians, we must have the Bible knowledge and the power of the Holy Spirit in us to know a poser when we meet one. A poser is a person who is one thing and pretends to be something else. If a person is not a Christian, but tries to act like one, he is a poser. I am not talking about someone who is new in Christ or is still learning and growing. I am talking about a person who acts like a Christian when it is convenient for him and acts like a heathen when that is convenient. I will give a couple of examples of what I mean. Suppose someone says they will only date Christians, so another person pretends to be a Christian so they can date them. Or suppose a person acts like a Christian in church, but in their business practices, they will cheat another person for an extra dollar or two. Another example is a person who acts like a Christian when others are watching, but when no one is looking they act totally different. You get the picture, and you may even be able to name a few examples of people you know.

In Matthew 7:21–23 we read "Not everyone who says to me, 'Lord, Lord,' will enter the kingdom of heaven, but only he who does the will of my father who is in heaven. Many will say to me on that day, 'Lord, Lord, did we not prophesy in your name, and in your name drive out demons and perform many miracles?' Then I will tell them plainly, 'I never knew you. Away from me, you evil doers.'"

Wow! What a glimpse into the day of judgment. But the most startling thing about this passage is that the people were calling Jesus "Lord" and even claiming to prophesy and do miracles *in His name*. They were claiming to be Christians and doing the Lord's work, but that is not what Jesus sees in them. He goes on to say that it is the person who **hears His** words and **puts them into practice** that will have a solid foundation in their lives. I'm sorry to say that there are people today in the church—even pastors and leaders who do this very thing. They do it without a fear of what they are doing and without thinking of the final consequences. They are blind guides leading the blind. If no one has the courage to step up and call them on it, they will continue. If I were a betting man, I would bet my last dollar that that man in the bar that night will never tell someone he's a member of a 1% club again. People will do what they think they can get away with. But if challenged, they will think twice.

One night a friend of mine went to a church service where a guest speaker was preaching. After the service, the preacher had prayer for people. During the prayer ceremony, he told my friend, who wore glasses, that his eyes were healed, and he did not need the glasses. To which my friend replied that if his eyes were healed, things would look fuzzy with his glasses on, and they did not. My friend was right, but the preacher just laughed and brushed him off. My friend was discouraged and went away sad.

I want everyone to know that I do believe in miracles, healing, and the power of God to touch people's lives. I have seen many miracles and many lives touched by God. However, as long as we are willing to put up with false people, false prophets, and false healing, the true miracles of God will be elusive. I know we do not like to be confrontational, but sometimes you just have to.

I want us to look at another passage of scripture in the book of Matthew. In these passages, Jesus is warning us of things to come in the last days, and what some of the signs will be of His coming. Matthew 24:4, 5 says, "Jesus answered; 'Watch out that no one deceives you. For many will come in my name, claiming, I am the Christ, and will deceive many.'" I have heard this passage preached many times warning of false christs coming and how they will be the anti-christ, but that is not at all what Jesus is saying. Read on, and I hope this will make sense to you. He is saying be on your guard that nobody deceives you. How are they going to be deceiving? By coming in His name. They're claiming to be Christians! Yes, those who call themselves "Christians" use His name to describe who and what they are.

The disciples were first called "Christians" in Antioch according to Acts11:26. At the time, they were actually making fun of them by calling them little Christ, because Barnabas and Saul spent a whole year there teaching them the things of Christ. They acted like Christ in all they did and they were called Christians.

They will not only come in His name in the last days, but they will also claim He, Jesus, is the Christ. Jesus did not say they would claim to be the Christ, but that they would claim that He was the Christ. Jesus is the one speaking in this passage when He says, *"they will come in My name claiming "I am the Christ."* Many will profess to be Christians and profess that Jesus is the Christ, but they will be posers. Not real Christians, but pretending to be, which throws others off the path of righteousness.

Sometimes people are pretenders because it is easier to do that, than make the commitment to the lifestyle they are imitating. I am pretty sure the man in the bar that night would have liked to be a 1% biker, but the cost was too great. The lifestyle was too challenging for him to live, but he wanted the accolades of being recognized as a 1% biker all the same. As children, we can all remember pretending to be a cowboy, a policeman, firemen, nurse, or even a doctor. There comes a time when we should grow out of those pretend characters and either become the real thing or move on to something we can be.

Paul, the Apostle, put it this way in 1 Corinthians 13:11: "When I was a child, I talked like a child, I thought like a child, I reasoned like a child. When I became a man, I put childish ways behind me." We, as people of God, must grow up and put off childish ways. It's time to be men and women of God without pretending to be something we are not. It's time to call the things that are unrighteous and ungodly what they are. It's time to require people of God to live like God's people.

I am going to close this chapter with one more example from the Bible: It's an account of someone who promised he would never deny Jesus even if everyone else did. Yes, the man is Peter, and it's an account of him trying to be something he was not. Shortly after Jesus was arrested and dragged away for crucifixion, we read in Matthew 26:69–74, "Now Peter was sitting out in the courtyard, and a servant girl came to him. 'You also were with Jesus of Galilee,' she said. But he denied it before them all. 'I don't know what you are talking about,' he said. Then he went out to the gateway, where another girl saw him and said to the people there, 'This fellow was with Jesus of Nazareth.' He denied it again, with an oath: 'I don't know the man!' After a little while, those standing there went up to Peter and said, 'Surely you are one of them, for your accent gives you away.' Then he began to call down curses on himself and he swore to them, 'I don't know the man!'"

You know the rest of the story. The rooster crowed three times, and Peter remembered Jesus' words that he would deny Him, and he went out and wept bitterly.

The things I notice about this account is that when we, like Peter, get away from our own people (Christians), it gets easier to pretend we are somebody else and we look for ways to hide who we really are. Then he went out to the gateway, trying harder to hide who he was, but sure enough somebody called him out on it. He denies it again, and this time with an oath, hoping that would convince them. After a little while Peter probably thought he was safe. *Whew! people starting to leave me alone.* Wrong Peter! It doesn't work for anyone who tries to deny who they really are! The thing that will usually give them away is their mouth. Those standing around Peter said **"*your accent gives you away.*"** That's right. His speech—his mouth gave him away, and that is the very thing that will give us all away when we try to hide who we are and pretend to be somebody or something we are not.

Peter even began to call down curses on himself trying to prove he was somebody he was not. It's amazing how far some will go to hide who they are. Would that the people of God be bold, speak up about who we are, and not be afraid to let others know that we know who they are.

Yes if only 1% of God's people would get what I call "Holy Ghost boldness" and not be ashamed of who they are and who they represent, we can change our nation and the church for the glory of God and His Kingdom.

FINAL THOUGHTS

I began this book by saying that I do not want to seem critical of the church. I know there are many great people of God out there trying their best to make a difference in the world and the church. I pray for you every day that the power of God would spread through your lives and ministries. I pray that God's Spirit would flow, not only through you, but from you. I know that even as I write this, there are Pastors who are struggling with small congregations and large congregations wanting to be able to do more for God and His people. There are some who are at what they believe to be the end of their rope and don't know what to do next. There are Pastors who face problems and feel they have nowhere to turn to for help. My friends, I want you to know that we are all in this together. There is nobody who walks alone in the Kingdom of God. Sometimes our pride is our own worst enemy, and we refuse to let anyone know how we hurt, or how at times we feel hopeless! We desperately need each other, especially in the times we live! The enemy is working overtime to kill, steal, and destroy the things of God. We must be vigilant, not quit and definitely not surrender to our circumstances. *Everything is subject to change!* Even the heavens and earth will pass away and a new one be created by God in it's place.

One of my favorite passages in the Bible is recorded in 2 Kings 7. The city of Samaria was under siege, and there seemed to be no hope of things getting better. The people were starving to death, but God had a different plan. In 2 Kings 7:1 we read, "Elisha said, 'Hear the word of the LORD. This is what the LORD says: About this time tomorrow, a seah of flour will sell for a shekel and two seahs of barley for a shekel at the gate of Samaria.'"

What the man of God was saying was that twenty-four hours from now things will be totally different; there would be plenty. And things *were* different! Praise God! You cannot imagine how many times in my own life I held on to this passage, knowing that God Almighty could change my circumstances. The same is true for many others in God's Kingdom. Whether you are a pastor, and serve God in that capacity, or you are serving God as a Christian right where you are, things will change. They will get better, for you and God's Church everywhere. If there is ever anything that I can do for you or your church I would be honored to do so whenever I can, or however I can. Do not hesitate to contact me. God Bless and remember ***Don't keep the faith—spread it!***

—Roger Bennett
One of God's 1% ers